Contents

Introduction

Revenue, fueled by a consistent flow of paying customers, is vital for any company. Effective sales teams, often overseen by sales managers, play a crucial role in achieving this. You'll gain insights and a systematic approach to create and manage a successful sales team. Whether you're establishing a new team or refining an existing one, you'll learn tools to recruit, motivate, deploy, and measure sales representatives. Explore the exciting field of sales management, develop essential skills, and embark on the journey to becoming an exceptional sales manager.

If you were a top-performing rep, you're likely eager to bring your talent and momentum to your new team. This book is here to support you in becoming a highly successful sales manager quickly and enjoyably. We'll cover starting on the right foot, setting the tone in meetings, coaching your team, and handling failures. Unlike typical training focused on improving sales skills, this book aims to enhance your leadership abilities. While being a sales manager can be challenging, it is also rewarding.

Enhance your sales effectiveness by developing and practicing empathy skills. Whether you're a division lead, manager, or team member, you will learn how to connect with prospects and clients on a deeper level. Empathy is the key to improving interpersonal connections, understanding, and relationships, crucial in the evolving market influenced by technological changes and accelerated business operations. We will empower you to achieve superior results in the rapidly changing sales landscape.

We will cover coaching, training, and the appraisal process, delving into revenue, expenses, and the role of customer relationship management software in enhancing key performance indicators. While challenging, mastering this responsibility is rewarding when it helps salespeople enhance their skills, boost sales, and maximize career opportunities.

Want a more motivated and inspired sales team, consistently performing at their best? You can achieve this without grand speeches. Discover how small adjustments can reset your team's psychological center, optimize your leadership moments, and boost a salesperson's energy even in just 10 seconds. Learn a language that enhances motivation, morale, and performance. Join me to elevate your team to the top tier of sales excellence.

Chapter 1 Sales Management Foundations

What is sales management?

Sales management is a cyclical process that begins with understanding the commercial marketing strategy, translating it into a clear sales task. This task outlines what sales representatives must do to succeed—identifying target customers, products, and sales methods. The next step involves structuring the sales team, recruiting top-notch talent, and establishing territories and quotas aligned with the sales task. Crafting an effective compensation program is crucial, as it influences various aspects of sales management. Measurement of results and accountability follow, focusing on key metrics tied to the sales task. This data, when fed back to the marketing team, informs adjustments to the commercial strategy, initiating the sales management cycle anew. Sales management is a disciplined, data-driven approach essential for sustained success amid tough competition.

Defining the sales task

Defining the sales task is the foundational and crucial first step in sales management. This involves answering four key questions: identifying target customers with precision, specifying the products and services to be sold, outlining the required selling activities, and establishing communication channels for support within the company. The more detailed and explicit the answers, the more effective and efficient the sales team becomes. Coordination between the sales manager and the marketing team is essential to ensure alignment. Throughout this book, the sales task will be emphasized due to its critical role in achieving success as a sales manager.

Recruiting salespeople

Recruiting top-notch sales reps is a crucial ongoing task for effective sales managers. To do this, start by creating a profile outlining the required skills, knowledge, and behaviors for the sales task. Collaborate with HR to develop a job description reflecting this profile and the duties outlined in the sales task. Potential recruits can be found within your company, through referrals, staffing agencies, universities, former military personnel, online job platforms, and traditional advertising. Conduct interviews using scripted questions focusing on the candidate's ability to perform specific aspects of the sales task. Two types of interview scripts are situation or behavior-based and performance-based. When you identify the right candidate, extend a fair and compelling employment offer, emphasizing their value to the team.

Conducting sales training

Creating a formal sales training program is crucial for the success of your sales team. Start by breaking down the sales task into a comprehensive list of specific skills, knowledge, and behaviors. If your recruits already possess some of these, the training should reinforce and fill in the gaps. For instance, a rep selling surgical instruments may need skills like call planning and product demonstration, knowledge of human anatomy and surgical procedures, and behaviors like being self-motivated and persuasive. Develop training modules for each item on these lists and choose effective trainers, such as star performers, sales managers, marketing managers, technical teams, or even customers. Consider the most impactful location for each module, whether in the field, at a customer's location, or online. Role-playing is a common and valuable aspect of sales training programs to ensure practical application of learned skills. A well-designed training program not only motivates reps but also demonstrates the company's commitment to their success, facilitating a fast start to building business.

Motivating salespeople

Motivating your sales team is a vital aspect of the sales manager's role, ensuring enthusiasm, reducing turnover, and maintaining productivity. Successful sales managers employ a mix of intrinsic and extrinsic rewards. Intrinsic rewards involve granting autonomy, emphasizing the value of products, and fostering a sense of loyalty. Extrinsic rewards encompass financial incentives, accolades, special titles, and recognition. Regular events and contests, along with involving reps in training and planning, contribute to motivation. Customer feedback is a powerful motivator, highlighting the direct impact of sales efforts. Recognizing successful reps publicly, involving them in various activities, and conducting sales contests all contribute to keeping them motivated, ultimately ensuring the success of the sales team.

Defining a sales force structure

Creating a sales structure involves determining the number of sales reps and their organization. Two approaches to determine the number of reps are the top-down and bottom-up methods. The top-down approach involves dividing the annual revenue goal by the average sales per customer and calculating the required number of reps. The bottom-up approach considers the total number of customers, their call frequency, and the reps' capabilities to determine the needed workforce. Once the number of reps is decided, organizing them by product focus, customer focus, or geography is essential. Utilizing a matrix that pairs products and customer types helps define the sales task for each combination, facilitating the organization of reps based on similarities in tasks across columns or rows. If all tasks are the same, organizing reps by geography is suitable.

Forecasting sales performance

To create territories, assess both market potential and sales potential. Market potential refers to the expected sales for the entire industry in the area, while sales potential is your company's share of that market. Forecasts can be based on objective data (historical performance) or subjective data (expert opinions). Two recommended approaches are the top-down method, starting with the national economic level, and the bottom-up method, where each sales rep estimates their territory's production, which is then aggregated to determine company-level sales potential.

Creating sales territories

To create sales territories, consider two methods: the buildup method and the breakdown method. The buildup method involves starting at the individual rep level, understanding their workload capacity, customer calls, and sales task requirements. For example, in the medical device sales scenario, reps may make about 500 calls per year, and geographical boundaries are drawn to allocate approximately 100 customers to each rep. In contrast, the breakdown method begins with the overall company sales potential forecast, dividing it by the number of reps to set expectations for each rep and then creating geographical territories based on this sales volume. Tips include using existing geographical boundaries, ensuring financial and IT systems support territory tracking, and being ready to adjust territory boundaries based on changing conditions. Well-designed sales territories contribute to customer satisfaction, cost efficiency, and enhanced rep motivation and productivity.

Setting sales quotas

A sales quota is a target amount that reps must sell, serving as a vital sales management tool to align reps with the company's strategy and sales task, focusing resources effectively and providing motivation. To set quotas, start by collecting data on each territory's market potential and the rep's sales history. Assess whether the rep is meeting, exceeding, or falling below the territory potential. Consider territory differences, adjusting quotas based on economic conditions, competition, and travel times. Tailor quotas to individual reps, considering factors like penetration levels and individual abilities. Recognize that not all reps will have the same quota, and adjust expectations for talent and territory conditions. Ensure quotas are fair, reasonable, and motivational, communicating them clearly to the reps. Quotas serve as a contract between the sales manager and the rep, signaling confidence in their ability to succeed.

Understanding sales compensation

To effectively manage a sales force, it's crucial to implement a compensation system that aligns with the market, encourages desired behaviors, and reflects the sales task at hand. The impact of compensation extends to the number and quality of sales calls, as well as the time reps dedicate to their roles. Tailoring the compensation plan to specific aspects of the sales task, such as target customers, products, success-driving activities, and interactions with other company departments, is essential. Developing a successful sales comp program requires collaboration with finance and human resource departments. A well-designed plan is simple, fair, flexible, affordable, and competitive. Evaluate the current compensation program, considering alignment with company strategy, affordability, competitiveness, and ease of administration. Seek diverse input from senior management, sales teams, support groups, and other relevant departments. Aim for simplicity and efficiency in administration, and ensure the plan is flexible and aligned with overall sales management goals. Successful sales managers invest time in designing a customized compensation plan that meets the specific needs of their company.

Designing sales compensation programs

To create a sales compensation program, follow these four steps. First, establish the annual earnings target for each sales rep, considering past performance, industry competitiveness, and potential adjustments. Second, choose a compensation method—whether a straight salary, variable commission, or a combination of both. Straight salary plans are simple but lack incentives, while variable commissions link earnings to sales but carry risk. Combination programs, offering a base salary plus commission, provide security and motivation. Third, set thresholds for earning variable income, such as fixed amounts, percentage of sales, or varied payments based on quotas. For example, a medical device rep might receive $3,000 per diagnostic machine for the first 10 units, increasing to $5,000 for units 11 to 20. Lastly, test the compensation program using previous year sales data to ensure alignment with earning expectations, desired behaviors, and simplicity. A well-crafted sales compensation program integrates with sales management elements, including the sales task, territory structure, quotas, and effective motivation for a successful outcome.

Communicating sales compensation

The best compensation plan requires effective communication. Create a formal written document detailing the plan, industry comparisons, and earning methods with examples. Coordinate with finance and HR for budget compliance. Conduct verbal presentations, announce the plan to the sales force, and follow up with one-on-one meetings for clarity, especially in special situations. Proper administration is crucial—provide continuous feedback, document calculations, adhere to pay schedules, and promptly resolve issues. Measure the plan against objectives and metrics for sales, profits, or market share. Continuously assess simplicity and proactively address any issues to ensure the plan's success.

Managing underperforming reps

Sales managers often encounter underperforming reps despite a robust compensation system. To address this, start by analyzing overall team performance through sales call reports and results. Evaluate whether reps are targeting the right accounts and if there are customer complaints. Diagnose underperformance by determining if the issue lies in a lack of skill or will. If the rep lacks the necessary skills, identify gaps and collaborate with training or HR for a customized remedial program. Ensure the rep acknowledges and commits to addressing the gaps. If the sales task has changed, review it with the rep and observe their performance in a sales call. Dealing with reps who know the job but aren't performing requires addressing potential issues like pay, motivation, or personal problems. Help the rep turn the situation around, setting clear limits and deadlines for improvement. If the deadlines aren't met, consider finding a replacement for that territory. Managing salespeople requires a personalized approach, recognizing individual differences in skills, motivations, and career goals. Effective managers address issues one person at a time.

Measuring sales performance

Sales managers ensure accountability by measuring both outputs and inputs of their team members. Outputs, such as sales revenue and new accounts, are assessed alongside inputs, like the number of calls and selling time per call. Utilizing ratios of inputs to outputs provides a more accurate evaluation. For example, comparing the ratio of sales calls to days worked reveals the efficiency of reps. Creating specific ratios for each activity contributes to a comprehensive sales effectiveness index. Meaningful measurements should focus on activities that impact performance, and evaluations should be continuous to enable timely corrective actions. Transparent communication about the evaluation criteria is crucial, fostering trust and demonstrating the manager's commitment to helping reps succeed through meaningful conversations and accurate data.

Creating the virtual sales task

Sales managers must be adaptable to changes in the marketplace, especially in today's evolving work environment. To update the sales task for virtual components, consider four key questions. First, reconsider the target customers, as virtual sales may provide access to different customer types. Second, evaluate the products and services, incorporating virtual technologies for enhanced support. Third, define activities for selling virtually, adjusting the number of virtual calls and considering what can be achieved in this context. Lastly, specify support departments for reps, ensuring guidelines to avoid unnecessary calls and maintain focus on essential selling tasks. The new world of virtual technologies presents opportunities to refine and optimize the sales task for effectiveness.

Conducting virtual competency programs

For an effective sales task with virtual components, ensure reps are proficient in virtual technologies. Setting high standards is crucial, mirroring professionalism in appearance and utilizing quality technology, including web cameras, microphones, and appropriate internet speed. Emphasize proper lighting and guide reps in creating a virtual selling studio with a quiet, well-acoustic environment. Teach etiquette for virtual calls, emphasizing no multitasking, eating, or distractions. Encourage good sales call planning, incorporating screen-sharing for documents, effective time management, and alignment with the sales task activities. Virtual sales calling presents opportunities and risks, and proactive training ensures reps excel in this aspect.

Creating virtual territories

Territories traditionally designate where sales reps operate, often geographically. However, in a virtual work environment, territories can be defined anywhere, presenting numerous possibilities and advantages. To establish virtual territories, assess the virtual sales task to determine reps' capacity for virtual calls, considering the absence of travel time. For instance, in a medical device scenario, reps making virtual calls can reach 1,000 calls per year, compared to 500 in person. This increased efficiency may reduce the required number of reps. Despite the benefits, it's crucial to proceed gradually, considering customer and rep adjustment. A hybrid approach, combining virtual and in-person visits, may ease the transition. Maintain some regional coherence in virtual territories to foster customer relationships and understanding. Consistently measure results, especially customer satisfaction, and periodically join reps on virtual sales calls. Collaborate with relevant internal teams, like IT and supply chain, to address logistical changes and optimize the benefits of virtual sales territories. Effective implementation relies on thoughtful leadership and cooperation.

Continuing your sales management journey

Sales managers are highly sought after for their crucial role in overseeing the sales force, a vital company asset. Effective sales managers yield optimal sales results, and the first-line sales manager is often deemed the most important position. To advance your career in sales management, consistently develop your professional skill set. Broaden your experience, possibly by transitioning to marketing roles like product or market development management. Seek opportunities abroad or in special projects to enhance your global and cultural knowledge. Embrace lifelong learning, staying updated on technology and industry best practices. Join professional communities, attend conferences, and engage in networking events to connect with other sales management professionals. Actively experiment with and reflect on new sales management techniques, aiming to learn faster than the rate of change. Maintain a strong ethical foundation, balancing business needs with individual concerns, communicating honestly, building trust, and prioritizing ethical practices. Successful sales managers earn respect through ethical leadership, not just accolades.

Chapter 2 Transitioning to Management for Salespeople

Defining a successful sales manager

Before transitioning to a sales manager role, you were likely a successful salesperson. However, excelling as a sales manager requires more than just strong sales skills. The key to setting yourself up for success in this new role is understanding its distinctions and recognizing where you can contribute the most value to your team.

Firstly, as a sales manager, you take on the role of a coach. Salesforce.com reports that combining sales training with field coaching quadruples sales productivity. This means your coaching has the power to significantly enhance your team's results. Effective coaching involves consistent field presence, providing constructive feedback, offering insights, and observing and assessing your team's skills and behaviors.

Secondly, successful communication is crucial as a sales manager. Your role as the leader puts your emails, phone calls, and meetings under scrutiny. To set the tone for effective team communication, focus on being concise, clear, and strategic. Your ability to communicate influences how your team interacts with each other and, ultimately, with customers.

Lastly, your scope extends beyond your office and your buyer's office. As a successful sales manager, you must broaden and deepen your understanding of the market. Your team will look to you for insights into future market trends, changes, successes, and challenges. Developing industry and business acumen is vital for success in your current role and positions you for future senior leadership roles.

In summary, prioritize coaching, communicate effectively, and expand your business acumen to become a successful sales manager quickly. While the role may be challenging, your capabilities have brought you to this position, and you are well-equipped to handle it.

Deprioritizing old skills

Not all exceptional salespeople automatically become successful sales managers, and there are reasons for this. Firstly, as a former salesperson, recognizing that different sales approaches are effective is crucial; avoid trying to create a team of clones and embrace diversity. Secondly, the administrative workload that comes with a managerial role can be frustrating, but establishing systems for handling administrative tasks is essential. Lastly, understanding that not everyone will perform at your level is important; variations in performance are common.

To overcome these challenges, focus on being an enthusiastic yet levelheaded leader. Your team will look to you for stability and the ability to handle challenges. Embrace the administrative aspect of your role by seeking advice from peers proficient in handling such tasks. Schedule ample time for coaching your team, as companies with more coaching hours experience higher win rates. As a new sales manager, set high expectations, communicate clearly, avoid frustration, and prioritize coaching and patience for long-term success.

Embracing your sales manager role

As a new sales manager, embracing leadership requires understanding its essence. Leadership isn't about sole decision-making or omniscience; it involves seeking help, learning, and growing. Connect with mentors, both at work and outside, to navigate your new role effectively. Be transparent with your team about your motivations and commitments, fostering trust and understanding. Clearly communicate expectations to avoid performance issues, and maintain an open door, welcoming feedback and learning from diverse perspectives. Leadership is a gradual process, so grant yourself the time to evolve.

Setting the tone as a sales manager

Leaders must establish the emotional tone for their teams, emphasizing the importance of a shared purpose. Many leaders overlook this crucial aspect, failing to recognize its impact on performance. When communicating with the team, carefully choose language to define the noble purpose of their work, consistently reiterating it. Rather than solely focusing on financial incentives, highlight the positive impact on customers' lives or businesses. Emphasizing customer impact engages the team's creativity and problem-solving abilities. Fear-based approaches have detrimental effects, leading to frantic behavior and negative customer experiences. To maintain a focus on a higher purpose, share customer stories regularly, illustrating the real impact of the team's solutions. Creating a work environment that fosters meaning and connection is crucial for effective leadership. The central theme throughout all aspects of leadership should be the profound impact on customers. This emphasis on customer impact not only enhances team performance but also aligns with the broader goals of pipeline management, sales coaching, and major accounts. Authenticity in conveying the commitment to customer success is key for leaders to inspire their teams.

Managing your team's sales pipeline

Managing the sales pipeline is critical for a sales team's success. New sales managers often find it challenging because they must oversee a shared pipeline with various customers at different stages, evaluated by the team. While the focus is typically on closing deals with prospects, neglecting lead generation and existing customers can have long-term consequences. Regular discussions with reps about leads, prospects, and customers are essential. Ask specific questions tailored to each pipeline stage to ensure a balanced approach and emphasize the overarching theme of customer impact. If concerned about the pipeline's quality, take proactive steps to address lead generation. Remember, the best time to address pipeline issues is now.

Coaching sales skills

As a new sales manager, coaching is a crucial part of your role. Unlike a sales assistant, a coach's objective is to enhance reps' independent success rather than intervening at every mistake. Effective coaching involves guiding reps through challenging scenarios, offering constructive feedback, and focusing on behaviors rather than just outcomes. Similar to coaching a child in hitting a baseball, emphasize essential behaviors like asking insightful questions for building value or networking for lead generation. Coaching is an ongoing, integral aspect of your role, requiring consistent effort for lasting improvement in results. Despite numerous responsibilities, coaching your team remains the most effective and enduring method for achieving better outcomes.

Supporting sales account management

In ongoing account management, it's essential for a sales manager to be involved both behind the scenes and occasionally in front of the customer.

While the rep primarily handles the account, the manager's presence can facilitate upsells, strengthen customer relationships, and help the rep engage with senior decision-makers. Joining calls provides opportunities to ask unique questions and coach the rep effectively. Regularly accompanying the rep in-person and coaching behind the scenes, especially during lengthy sales cycles, enhances the chances of closing deals successfully.

Hiring and managing sales talent

New sales managers often aspire to build an A team of superstars, but the reality is that finding such individuals within budget constraints can be challenging. It's crucial to recognize that not everyone is suited for sales, and a person's success in other areas doesn't guarantee success in sales. During interviews, it's essential to look beyond immediate qualifications. For example, when comparing two candidates, the one without direct experience but demonstrating a strong work ethic and genuine enthusiasm for the company's purpose might be the better hire. Remember, product and industry knowledge can be taught, but work ethic and passion are crucial traits that candidates should bring to the table from the start. If a candidate lacks these qualities, it's best to consider other options.

Dealing with bad sales talent

As a new sales manager, if you didn't choose your team, effective coaching becomes crucial. However, some underperforming reps may not be fixable and can have negative consequences for the team and your brand. If a bad rep is costing more than just missed sales, and you have the authority, it's time to consider termination. If termination isn't an option, focus on neutralizing the underperformer by working on easier-to-change behaviors, such as call openings or email correspondence. Avoid giving them the toughest customers, as this can worsen their performance and damage your reputation. Instead, showcase good examples by utilizing star players on your team. In some cases, accepting that a poor performer may not change overnight and reallocating your time to more promising areas may be necessary.

Scheduling sales meetings

Enduring yet another meeting that could have been an email is a common frustration. When deciding whether a meeting is necessary, consider the scenario. For topics like new sales support materials, sending them in advance and conducting interactive discussions is more effective than everyone merely reviewing them during a meeting. Welcoming a new employee can justify a brief meeting, fostering a personal connection. Conversely, for issues like late expense reports, addressing individuals privately is more productive than a group meeting. Losing a significant account merits a private meeting first to address the responsible reps, followed by a group meeting for lessons learned and future strategies. The pattern is clear: if information can be communicated via email, it's likely more efficient than convening a meeting. Meetings should be reserved for fostering positive emotions, problem-solving, idea generation, and discussing plans, as time is a valuable resource for you and your sales team. Therefore, before calling a meeting, carefully assess if gathering people for a face-to-face discussion is truly essential.

Determining the best type of sales meeting

For an effective meeting, it's crucial to understand different types of meetings. A creative brainstorming meeting involves facilitating discussions on new sales strategies or networking techniques. Your role is to guide the conversation and ensure clear action steps. Information sharing meetings focus on generating enthusiasm and making facts actionable, especially for new products or leadership changes. Meetings for communicating expectations, whether positive or negative, create a shared understanding among the team. Implementing weekly huddles, whether virtual or in person, boosts team speed and accountability. Regardless of the meeting type, have a defined agenda and clear outcomes to avoid the frustration of aimless gatherings. Before calling a meeting, clarify your goals and what success looks like, informing the content and agenda responsibilities.

Setting the tone for sales team meetings

There are two common meeting mistakes: treating them as a one-way information transfer and lacking clear action items. To avoid these pitfalls, use a tight agenda that outlines discussion topics, input needed, and decisions to be made. For instance, when addressing a sales target shortfall, structure the agenda to explore reasons, strategies, and key action items. Communicate from the start that the meeting will be interactive, promoting discussion and decision-making. This approach is effective in both positive and challenging situations, fostering an all-inclusive atmosphere and emphasizing collective accountability.

Involving customers in sales meetings

Shift the focus of sales meetings from internal targets to customer-centric discussions by involving customers both physically and metaphorically. Physically, introduce customers to your office environment, allowing employees to see the real faces behind their work. This is especially beneficial for non-customer-facing staff, fostering connection and boosting confidence. Engage customers in sales meetings to gain insights into their world, asking about their buying motivations, potential shifts to competitors, business goals, industry outlook, and challenges. For remote teams, utilize video conferencing to bring customers into the discussion. Figuratively, employ techniques like Jeff Bezos's empty chair, prompting consideration of customer impact in decision-making. Incorporate customer testimonials and success stories to continually reinforce the focus on customer impact, reminding reps that the ultimate goal is the positive effect on customers.

Utilizing guests in your sales team meetings

Consider bringing in specific individuals to enhance your sales meetings:

1. Product Development Representative: Establish a peer-to-peer relationship with someone from the product development team to stay informed about updates and share field feedback. This collaboration benefits both sides and contributes significantly to your team's knowledge.

2. Marketing Representative: Invite a marketing professional to gain insights into key messages, exciting initiatives, and strategies that resonate with potential customers. Instead of complaining about lead quantity, focus on building a positive relationship, obtaining support, and understanding how sales can contribute to the brand.

3. Your Boss: Once trust and rapport are established with your team, consider inviting your boss to join meetings. Use this opportunity to showcase your team's achievements rather than trying to impress your boss. Authentic examples of your team's wins will naturally reflect positively on you.

Avoid inviting individuals who may drain the energy from the meeting with uninteresting or irrelevant presentations. If someone insists on presenting, suggest alternative methods like PowerPoint or online delivery and coach them to make their content action-oriented, ensuring that meetings focus on progress and motivation.

Working with marketing

Successful business outcomes depend on both sales and marketing. In today's landscape, even industries like consulting, engineering, and software sales, traditionally built on one-on-one relationships, rely heavily on online buyer experiences shaped by marketing efforts. As a new sales manager, it's crucial to grasp the synergy between sales and marketing. Marketing addresses the many, creating brand awareness and fostering audience receptivity, while sales focus on individual interactions. Avoid the common mistake of siloing or competing sales and marketing within your organization. Instead, build a collaborative relationship by understanding what marketing does, their objectives, and how they are evaluated. Rather than complaining, study marketing, learn their language, and emphasize collective customer experiences and brand essence when communicating with them. This collaborative approach enhances your understanding of the entire buyer's journey and positions you as an ally to the marketing team.

Working with accounting

Sales is more than just numbers; it's about customer impact. However, understanding the financial aspects of your organization is crucial as a sales manager. Maintaining a good relationship with the finance team is essential. Your knowledge of the financials, such as product profitability and customer value, distinguishes you as a potential senior leader. While your strengths may lie in people skills, grasping finance, the language of business, is key. Familiarize yourself with revenue sources, fixed costs, net margin, and ROI. Finance plays a vital role in billing and collections with customers, so fostering goodwill with the finance team is advised. Follow three rules: grasp the organization's financial big picture, learn financial language, and cultivate positive relationships with finance professionals.

Working with product

Product development is vital for future success. As a sales manager, you play a crucial role in influencing your company's future by providing valuable customer information to the product development team. Instead of just relaying complaints or wish lists, strive to understand trends within collective customer feedback. As you interact with multiple customers on the front line, focus on discerning their key business issues, desires, and challenges. Share this insightful intel with your product team to enhance their understanding. Additionally, encourage your product team to engage directly with customers to witness product usage and gather valuable insights. Your ability to offer customer intelligence is key to both your success and the organization's. Bringing product teams closer to customers benefits everyone involved.

Communicating effectively with senior leaders

When interacting with senior leaders, it's crucial to make a lasting impression. Instead of solely highlighting past achievements, take a strategic approach. Ask thoughtful questions about key business areas, demonstrate your team's capabilities, and express eagerness for new challenges. Emphasize your passion for customer success, focusing on the broader impact in a positive way. Keep communications concise and strategic, making the most of your limited face or screen time with senior leaders.

Managing a personal failure

Failure is a universal experience, often accompanied by physical and emotional distress, especially when it becomes public, which is likely in a sales manager role. To cope with failure, recognize it as an integral part of success. Understand that big achievements often involve numerous failures. Acknowledging failure is crucial; avoiding defensiveness and redirecting energy towards solutions is key. Embrace failures as part of the process, learn from them, and take public responsibility when necessary. Avoid dwelling on the mistake and encourage open communication within the team for continuous improvement. Remember, failure doesn't define you; your ability to rebound, learn, and move forward does.

Managing a sales team failure

Just as you and your team will experience failures, how you handle your team's failures is crucial for their resilience. When someone on your team makes a mistake, avoid addressing it publicly. Privately meet with them to understand their perspective and assess their awareness of the situation. If they're self-aware, focus on problem-solving. If not, ask impact questions to help them grasp the broader consequences. Assure them that you're on their side and emphasize the goal of understanding and learning to prevent future mistakes. Encourage them to think about what they would do differently next time. Provide clear guidance for moving forward, fostering an environment that acknowledges failure, learns from it, and emerges with a stronger commitment to success.

Navigating unexpected failure

Sometimes failures occur that aren't your or your team's fault, like external economic conditions or unforeseen product issues. As a leader, taking responsibility is essential, even when you're not directly to blame. Mary Barra, the CEO of GM, faced a crisis with ignition switch defects causing customer deaths shortly after her promotion. Despite not causing the problem, she assumed responsibility, initiated a thorough examination of the failure, and committed to creating a new organizational culture. This approach, acknowledging and addressing failure regardless of fault, is a powerful model for leaders in various roles. In challenging times, leaders who candidly assess reality without assigning blame emerge stronger. When confronted with failure, confront the situation, acknowledge the reality, and decide on a proactive course of action.

Furthering your skills as a sales manager

You were chosen as a sales manager for a reason. If you currently possess about 60% of the skills needed, that's sufficient. Growth into the role is part of the process. No one becomes a CEO, president, or general fully prepared. Embrace the support around you—your team, colleagues, boss, customers, and family all want your success. It's not about being perfect; it's about receiving assistance. As a sales manager, shift your focus from yourself to your team's success. Recognize your role as the crucial link between your reps and company management. Three key aspects: prioritize your team over yourself, invest in coaching and developing your team, and don't fear failure—it's part of sales management.

Chapter 3 Empathy in Sales

Understanding why empathy matters

Empathy involves understanding and connecting with others, a crucial skill in both personal and professional contexts. Consider a scenario where interns witnessed layoffs at a financial services company, impacting their perception of the workplace. Empathy, often viewed as a soft skill, is essential for adapting responses and developing suitable plans based on an understanding of others' experiences. Applying empathy in professional interactions, whether with colleagues or clients, enhances communication, collaboration, and relationship building. Taking an empathetic approach can significantly improve outcomes and create a positive cycle of understanding and cooperation. Try incorporating empathy into your next conversation to experience the benefits in your interactions and results.

Sales impact from using empathy

Consider the changes in the sales process over the past five years. Previously, sellers held more power and information, but technology advancements have shifted dynamics. Buyers now have extensive information about products and competitors before engaging with sellers. Sales teams connect with buyers later in the process, and increased noise requires adjustments in sales strategies. Collaboration within teams and empathy skills are crucial in navigating these changes. Incorporating empathy into research and outreach enhances understanding, builds trust, and improves solution proposals. The ability to read and connect with people is key to success in the evolving sales landscape.

Discovering how empathy works

After a disappointing sales call, John shares his frustration, and you respond with empathy, showcasing the power of understanding others' emotions. Our brains have mirror neurons that trigger shared emotions, motivating us to act. This empathetic behavior is fundamental for collaboration and reciprocity. There are three empathy components: cognitive (understanding perspectives), affective (shared emotional response), and empathetic concern (acting based on the other person's experience). Actively practicing empathy in sales improves results by addressing concerns, understanding needs, and building trust, benefiting both external interactions and team dynamics.

Leading with empathy

A top sales manager at HubSpot prioritizes hiring individuals with empathy and genuine interest in the company's products for authentic connections with prospects and customers. The hiring process emphasizes behavioral questioning to assess collaboration skills, as the lone wolf approach is discouraged. Leadership styles at HubSpot adapt to new conditions, emphasizing cultural elements that foster psychological safety, open discussion, and collaboration. Fear-based and ego-driven tactics are replaced with coaching approaches that emphasize listening and observing. Sales leaders should use empathy to understand how team members are adjusting to a fast-paced environment and offer individualized support. Model relevant behavior, utilize coaching moments, and encourage the practice of empathy to enhance team interactions and customer relationships.

Improving performance with empathy

Are your early morning weekly meetings optimal for everyone? Instead of post-work drinks, are there more effective ways to build team cohesion? Some team members may be missing out due to consistent absences. Empathy is crucial for understanding your team, enabling each member to excel in sales and foster effective teamwork. Adapting to market changes and evolving work environments requires increased engagement throughout the sales process. Recognize and accommodate individual differences in working styles and preferences using empathy. Adjust team practices accordingly, such as rescheduling meetings for those not at their best in the mornings or organizing team-building events at different times. Leverage empathy to identify and capitalize on individual strengths and skills, aligning tasks with employees' enjoyment and proficiency. Gallup indicates that focusing on strengths increases engagement and positively impacts sales and profits. Identify team members' current and desired skills with empathy, ensuring competitiveness and adapting to evolving business needs. Lastly, encourage the use of empathy in interactions to strengthen internal collaboration and enhance external conversions. Utilize empathetic understanding to boost individual productivity and overall team results.

Distributing team responsibility

Technological advancements have significantly increased the availability of data, not only on prospects and customers but also on the effectiveness of the products or services your team sells. Broad, vague outcomes are no longer sufficient, and accountability for sales professionals has risen with the digitization of business. Specific data collection allows for quick testing, sharing outcomes, updating targets, and refining parameters. Customers now expect these steps to complete the sales cycle and justify future sales. When assigning new responsibilities based on information requirements, use empathy to clarify expectations and ensure team members understand precise needs from prospects, clients, and management. Provide explicit, detailed direction to avoid misinterpretations. Sensitize your assessment of team members with empathy, adapting your approach based on individual comfort with new methods and tools. Address specific support needs, such as extra training for those struggling with data-rich tools. In the ongoing sales process, practice empathy to motivate and monitor each team member individually, especially when dealing with complex ad sales. Tailor assistance to help each person develop their unique angle and value. Tap into the team's energy and emotions to rally them for optimal results.

Providing team empathy training

The head of sales at Fuse emphasized the importance of empathy to his teams, coaching them to understand their prospects' perspectives. In a competitive market, providing empathy training is crucial to help teams recognize its value and improve results. Highlight the integral role of empathy in the sales process, particularly in adapting to data, tools, and technology advances. Illustrate how empathy enables sales reps to understand business needs, appreciate perspectives, and establish credibility. Encourage team members to participate fully in training by using metrics that resonate with them, showcasing successful outcomes with empathetic practices. Establish a common language around empathy within the organization, focusing on terms that resonate with team members. Emphasize the importance of emotional intelligence (EQ) and regularly reinforce empathetic practices to create a more inclusive and supportive team environment. Make empathy training a natural choice by consistently demonstrating its powerful effects.

Increasing sales using empathy

The VP of Sales at Workfront emphasizes the importance of an empathetic approach in successful sales tactics. Rather than focusing solely on what is said, she encourages her team to listen actively and uncover the pain points of potential customers. Successful team members demonstrate a drive to help customers succeed, bringing empathy and passion to their work. Active listening, open-ended questions, and empathetic responses deepen understanding and connection. This approach builds trust and allows for more impactful recommendations, addressing the root causes of customers' challenges. By demonstrating authentic intention and empathy, sales professionals can boost their success in connecting with and satisfying customers.

Adopting key empathy habits

In the challenging landscape of financial services, client acquisition and retention demand careful consideration. The integration of empathy into the sales process is crucial for success. Implementing a three-step approach—think, feel, and act—can enhance every phase of the process. First, consciously consider the prospect's point of view, understanding their challenges and tailoring communications accordingly. Second, empathize with the client's emotions and experiences to propose relevant solutions and build meaningful relationships. Finally, use this understanding to create a customized solution that precisely addresses their pain points, increasing the likelihood of conversion and client satisfaction. Practicing empathy throughout the entire sales process significantly improves outcomes.

Deepening customer relationships

Beyond closing a sale, the benefits of empathy extend to long-term customer relationships and upselling opportunities. Strengthen connections by building on common personal and professional points identified during initial interactions. Relate experientially and emotionally to deepen the bond through shared experiences. Utilize empathy skills, such as active listening and asking open questions, to encourage clients to open up about their interests. Find creative ways to connect, even within constraints like cost or regulations in financial services. Invest time in nurturing relationships, creating lasting memories, and staying informed about clients' situations. Apply empathy to adapt solutions over time, proactively learning from successes and challenges. Practice the three empathy skills—think, feel, act—to positively impact client understanding and relationships. Getting to know your clients better enhances both business and personal satisfaction.

Promoting sales team results

Fuze's high-performing team fosters collaboration and mutual support, sharing insights and congratulating each other after client interactions. HubSpot and a bank's sales team also emphasize the importance of team dynamics in their success. Collaborating within a sales team is crucial for achieving shared goals. Recognize and appreciate diverse styles and talents within the team, encouraging empathy to understand and share successful approaches. Access a range of perspectives by connecting with team members' experiences and methods. Use empathy to offer support when a team member faces challenges or needs advice. Foster collaboration by pairing up team members with complementary skills. Apply an empathetic approach to understand your team members' strengths and challenges, offering assistance where needed. Support each team member's success through empathetic interactions, enhancing overall team results and making the work more enjoyable.

Nurturing empathetic relationships

When hiring new team members, focus on qualities that promote relationship-building, emphasizing empathy and strong interpersonal skills. Recognize the increasing importance of relationships, communication, and emotional intelligence in sales recruiting. Foster a supportive work environment that encourages positive interactions and consistent experiences, both in-person and virtually. Lead by example, highlighting the benefits of thoughtful interactions and meaningful relationships. Organize regular team-building activities, tailored to each team's culture and preferences, to enhance connections. Schedule regular non-work-related conversations and virtual hangouts to nurture relationships, especially for remote teams. Proactively create conditions conducive to building, deepening, and maintaining relationships within the team. Block time for team members to learn about each other's interests, families, and passions, facilitating better collaboration and support.

Bridging differences with empathy

A disconnect between boomer senior management and millennial frontline workers at a toxic waste cleanup company led to conflicts and reduced productivity. Empathy helped executives understand the concerns and valuable ideas of younger employees, leading to increased productivity. In sales, connecting across diverse mediums and locations requires deliberate efforts. Practice empathy by finding common ground through shared experiences and thoughtful questions. Align with teammates mentally by focusing on shared views and enjoying non-work-related experiences together. Clear delineations can prevent conflicts among team members, when necessary, use empathy to resolve conflicts by understanding and acknowledging each other's perspectives. Recognize the diversity in backgrounds and generations, and practice empathy internally to reduce differences and strengthen relationships within the team. Extend the same effort to prospects and improve overall interactions.

Encouraging open-mindedness

A senior sales manager in financial services prioritizes recruiting sales reps with strong interpersonal skills and an open-minded, curious mindset. This combination predicts success in developing networks, converting prospects, and fostering teamwork. Prioritizing open-mindeness reinforces cultural values of openness and inclusion, promoting psychological safety within the team. Emphasizing inclusion encourages diverse perspectives in brainstorming sessions, leading to enhanced creativity and outcomes. In team meetings, practicing inclusive language and building upon others' ideas helps overcome groupthink and encourages positive affirmation. In brainstorming sessions, using the "Yes, and?" or "Good, interesting idea, and?" approach fosters a collaborative environment where creative ideas flourish. Aligning everyone with a focus on the customer journey and adopting an open-minded and empathetic approach ensures that sales interactions are positive, productive, and inclusive.

Avoiding empathy blockers

Take responsibility for fostering a culture of empathy and support by proactively addressing attitudes or approaches that hinder empathetic exchanges. Start by examining your own mindset, internal dialogue, and comments to others. Recognize the impact of judgments and assumptions, which can block empathy. Instead, seek clarity on the other person's experience or perspective, adjusting your understanding accordingly. Acknowledge and set aside your initial reactions to focus on the other person's experience. Encourage others to do the same by noticing their reactions and setting an example. Be aware of your emotions, recognize moments of judgment, step back from your feelings, and prioritize understanding others. This heightened empathy will contribute to your success as a sales professional.

Establishing empathetic sales habits

Sales environments often rely on fear, shame, and individual celebrations, which can motivate only a few people in the long term and hinder collaboration essential for successful teams. To transform behaviors, it's crucial to define empathy, highlight its impact, and consistently model empathetic behavior and language. Give your team permission to adopt new ways of behaving and speaking, introducing a cadence and language that aligns with your company's culture. Implement habits focusing on empathy's think, feel, and act steps, supported by relevant tools. Foster perspective-taking routines and practices that tune into people's experiences, encouraging active listening and connection. Establish regular routines for personal engagement and relationship-building. Track, measure, and reward new empathetic behaviors to reinforce team commitment and improve overall results. Regularly survey teams, reward success stories, and make necessary adjustments or additions to training. Embrace and model empathy habits to establish and sustain a productive and empathetic sales force.

Chapter 4 Sales Performance Measurement and Reporting

Coaching and training your sales team

Our success relies on the quality of the products/services we sell and the effectiveness of our sales team. While revenue targets and performance metrics are crucial, our responsibility extends to coaching and training our team. This begins from the day of hiring, requiring a well-planned training program covering sales processes, product knowledge, collaborative selling, communication, financial aspects, and individual coaching. We must actively lead and own these training efforts to ensure our team's success. Additionally, making tough decisions promptly is vital for continuous improvement. Establishing a robust training and coaching regimen is a critical management responsibility that directly influences the effectiveness of our sales team and, consequently, our own performance evaluation.

Drafting objectives for your sales direct report

What are your thoughts on using personal objectives as a performance metric? In my opinion, collaborating with salespeople to create focused and actionable objectives is an opportunity for productive coaching. While some prefer structured and formal corporate requirements, I believe in keeping it simple with fewer, more achievable objectives. Many endorse the SMART strategy—Specific, Measurable, Achievable/Agreed, Relevant/Realistic, Trackable/Time Limit—for effective objective-setting. This approach fosters collaboration, ensures clarity, and promotes ownership. Developing agreed-upon objectives with measurable outcomes can enhance teamwork, coaching efforts, and skill improvement for each sales professional.

Using your performance appraisal process to grow skills

Performance appraisals, though often viewed as bureaucratic, remain a key evaluation element in many companies. While some have eliminated them, it's crucial to work within company requirements and seek ways to improve the process. Regular, quarterly discussions integrated into overall management plans can make appraisals more effective. Communication is essential, and linking coaching and training with performance management creates a teamwork approach. Setting objectives collaboratively, evaluating regularly, and celebrating achievements fosters a positive outlook. The performance appraisal process, when thoughtfully handled, becomes an opportunity to enhance the skills of each salesperson, ultimately tying back to the key objective of increasing revenue and profits.

Building effective incentive plans, compensation, and contests for your sales team

Incentive plans, compensation programs, and contests are powerful motivators for sales teams, offering opportunities for increased earnings. However, their implementation requires careful design, clear communication, and fairness across the organization. Managing someone's finances in performance measurement can be stressful, necessitating a focus on increasing revenue while ensuring equitable rewards. Effective incentive plans set achievable targets and motivate salespeople, with simplicity being key for measurement success. Salary reviews, traditionally tied to year-end processes, are now often influenced by corporate controls, posing challenges as a performance measure. Contests, such as spiffs, offer immediate rewards for specific achievements within set periods, enhancing motivation and focus. Collaboration with human resources and financial teams is essential to navigate legal rules and ensure budget alignment. Well-tuned incentive structures positively impact sales performance when managed effectively.

Setting and communicating your sales target strategy

Setting sales targets, while stressful, is crucial. It involves collaboration and careful consideration of individual performance, account dynamics, and overall business health. Communicating the sales target strategy clearly is essential. Monitoring sales performance, once a manual task, has evolved with advanced customer relationship management software, providing real-time results and allowing consistent tracking. While various KPIs are important, hitting individual quotas remains the key driver of success or disappointment.

Expense targets

Expense tracking is crucial for sales organizations, ensuring profitability alongside revenue. Key expense items include travel, marketing, sales meetings, training, technology, and salary/benefits. Building close ties with the finance department is essential for effective budgeting. Managing expenses, measured through the sales to cost ratio, is as vital as achieving revenue goals. This performance management aspect distinguishes successful sales organizations from unprofitable ones.

Trackable sales metrics: KPIs

With updated corporate systems and customer relationship management software, tracking numerous KPIs is now possible. While it's great to have detailed metrics, the primary focus should always be on revenue versus quota. Educating everyone on the terminology is crucial for effective communication. Commonly tracked KPIs include revenue, expenses, leads, lead response time, opportunities, new accounts opened, close win rate, actual deal size, sales cycle length, and sales representative ranking. The danger lies in analyzing too much data, as revenue versus quota remains the critical KPI that drives business success or disappointment.

Close and win rates

The most crucial performance metric is the actual number of sales closed. This metric, after the summary of total revenue attained, holds significance because it directly reflects a salesperson's success and ties into various aspects of the organization. Calculating the close rate can be done by evaluating the number of deals closed versus the number of opportunities in the pipeline, while the win rate considers the revenue estimate from all opportunities against the actual revenue achieved when sales are closed. Both ratios are valuable for analysis. Close/win rates are key indicators that tie into coaching, training, and leadership effectiveness.

The manager's coaching and training influence how well sales representatives follow the sales process, handle objections, and close deals. Leadership style plays a role in motivation and team success. Additionally, product or service issues impacting sales outcomes, competitive factors, and the collaborative effort of the team should be considered when evaluating close/win rates. While modern systems provide extensive metrics, it's crucial not to lose focus on this indicator, which is closely linked to revenue and provides a comprehensive view of the organization's effectiveness in providing solutions to customers. Close/win rates separate talkers from real producers and demand ongoing attention as a key performance indicator.

Customer relationship management software

Before the advent of Customer Relationship Management (CRM) software, salespeople stored account information in various formats, leading to unsophisticated tracking and subjective performance reviews. Today, with increased competitiveness, sharing detailed account data through CRMs is essential. CRMs offer key benefits for evaluation:

1. Centralized Information: Leads, opportunities, close rates, and more are consolidated in one location, replacing scattered databases and spreadsheets.

2. Forecasting: CRMs streamline forecasting by providing everyone's numbers weighted by potential close rates, enhancing accuracy and speed.

3. Market Feedback: CRMs enable consistent data input, facilitating quality feedback from sales professionals and easy retrieval for managers and other departments.

4. Channel Analysis: Efficient measurement of accounts by channel, including resources spent, revenue achieved, and cost-to-sales ratios.

5. Teamwork and Engagement: CRMs encourage collaboration among departments to focus on providing solutions to customers, reinforcing this crucial objective.

However, successful CRM implementation requires reinforcement and usage requirements from companies, with managers modeling usage and providing feedback. When integrated with revenue and expense reporting, a CRM provides a comprehensive view of the business, individual sales representatives, channels, and accounts, making it an indispensable tool for performance management analyses.

Dashboards

There are excellent tools like account tracking, sell-through reporting, and customer relationship management software. However, the abundance of data has led to complaints of overload. Establishing a reporting and measurement strategy for key performance indicators (KPIs) is crucial. Dashboards, visual displays of tracked metrics, are an effective way to organize and present data in a user-friendly manner. They can be customized for various business needs. Examples include:

1. Snapshot Dashboard: Displays basic information like sales, account tracking, and new accounts opened for a quick business status report.

2. Consolidated Dashboard: Offers more summarized details, including individual salespeople, year-to-date summaries, and other KPIs, customizable for specific teams or channels.

3. Complex Dashboard: Tracks about 10 items in a well-designed format, providing a comprehensive view of the business for sales or marketing professionals.

4. Leads, Opportunities, Closed Sales Dashboard: Focuses on the pipeline, allowing quick assessment of progress from lead to closed sale, highlighting potential issues.

The availability of extensive sales and marketing information from various systems represents significant advancements in the past decade. Starting the day with a sales dashboard provides a quick overview of the business, enhancing awareness and professionalism when refined, improved, and shared across the organization.

Customer feedback

Positive customer feedback is a key performance indicator (KPI) for evaluating sales success, company performance, and product/service acceptance. While customer feedback is valuable, it's just one aspect of the overall performance evaluation. Objective data, obtained through methods like account visits, business reviews, and industry conventions, complements subjective feedback. Surveys can provide objective insights, but caution and expertise are needed in their development and analysis. Direct sales results, such as rankings among territories, offer indirect objective feedback, signaling areas for improvement in sales, coaching, training, or product/service offerings. Customer feedback is crucial, but understanding its variables is essential for a comprehensive performance evaluation. Regularly asking questions and attentively listening to accounts is an ongoing responsibility in the assessment process.

Effective use of promotions with accounts

The evaluation of how salespeople utilize promotions and collateral material is often viewed subjectively. To improve this process, a thorough review of created materials, budget allocation, and collaboration among sales, business development, finance, and marketing management is crucial. Tracking systems can help measure the effectiveness of marketing programs and a salesperson's utilization. Examples include cooperative advertising, marketing fund usage, response to deals/offers, social media engagement, and sell-through analysis. Regular training on expense management and assessing ROI ensures that promotional efforts align with revenue growth objectives. Ultimately, the effectiveness of marketing materials relies on understanding customer needs and maximizing their impact on sales, a key performance measure mastered by top salespeople.

Next steps

Sales management involves numerous responsibilities, and one crucial skill is evaluating and measuring individual and departmental sales performance. With advanced tools like account tracking systems and CRMs, detailed analysis is possible through visually appealing dashboards, covering leads, opportunities, forecasts, and personal objectives. Amidst this complexity, the core responsibility remains addressing customer needs with products or services, directly tied to the key metrics of closed sales and total revenue achieved. Effective performance measurement supports decision-making for continuous improvement. Investing time in this process yields positive outcomes.

Chapter 5 How to Motivate Your Sales Teams

Declare your noble purpose

Want financial success and to make a meaningful impact? Good news – you don't have to choose. Sales is a noble profession, driven by solving customer problems and building relationships. Purpose-driven salespeople, focused on improving lives, outperform their transactional counterparts by over 350%. Research shows that salespeople aiming to make a difference are more adaptable and resilient. While competitive compensation is crucial, a noble purpose beyond quotas sustains motivation. Craft a purpose statement for your team, drawing inspiration from customer testimonials and team members. It guides your team, clarifies impact, and fuels motivation for lasting success.

Set the psychological center

In the fast-paced world of sales, maintaining a stable psychological center is crucial for your team's success. Without it, they may lurch between highs and lows, impacting customer interactions negatively. To ground your team, shift their focus from closing deals to making a difference for customers. Use the game-changing question: "How will this customer be different as a result of doing business with us?" Incorporate it in pipeline reviews, discussions about wins, and product introductions. Avoid generalizations; discussing the impact on individual customers is more potent. By making customer impact a consistent theme, you reinforce the significance of your team's work.

How to get clear on sales compensation

The way you present compensation can either motivate or frustrate your team. Many organizations use a carrot-and-stick approach, thinking incentives and bonuses will drive performance. However, excessive incentives and constant plan changes may lead to short-term activity but rarely improve skills. Changing comp plans frequently takes up mental space, creates inconsistency, and can result in unethical behavior. Even if you don't control the comp plan, how you discuss it matters. Be detail-oriented, prompt with updates, and emphasize that compensation follows making a difference for customers. Addressing complex issues prevents salespeople from leaving solely over compensation, fostering confidence and commitment to achieving goals.

Define the win for your sales team

Define a win for your team beyond a closed deal; it's about sticky deals closing at high margins based on value-based relationships. Instead of a generic celebration, provide specific details about the win. For instance, if Jane closed a deal, elaborate on her efforts, such as multiple discovery conversations, insightful questions, and connecting the customer's needs with our solution. Highlight the positive impact on the customer and emphasize that replicating such wins involves specific behaviors, like deep discovery and value building. This approach builds a replicable process for the entire team, fostering sustainable growth and leaving everyone, team and customers, feeling great.

Establish a learning mindset with your sales team

Continuous learning is crucial in the ever-changing business landscape, especially in sales. Linking learning to motivation creates a loop of improvement: learn, apply, succeed. To foster a learning mindset, encourage ongoing improvement, responsiveness to feedback, and team support. Effective sales coaching, particularly with high performers, yields significant returns. Utilize diverse learning resources, including external materials and peer coaching, to maximize coaching efficiency. As a leader, model a commitment to learning, demonstrating its ongoing importance. Sustaining a team learning mindset involves strategic coaching and transparently showcasing your own commitment to continuous learning.

Leverage your sales leadership airtime

The way you use your leadership airtime significantly influences what your team considers important. For sales leaders, emphasizing only numbers creates a narrow narrative, risking team members feeling like mere cogs. To build a deep belief in your team, use leadership airtime to share customer impact stories, celebrate team wins, discuss industry changes, and provide valuable insights or strategies. Wisely allocate your leadership airtime to inspire and uplift your team, reinforcing the broader purpose beyond numbers.

Share customer impact stories to ignite frontal lobes

Storytelling is vital for both securing significant deals and motivating your team for future successes. Customer impact stories, different from traditional case studies and win stories, highlight the meaningful impact your team has on individuals or businesses. These stories, typically under three minutes, incorporate specific details like names and locations while emphasizing emotion and impact. For instance, Hootsuite's customer impact story during Hurricane Sandy illustrates how their solution aided New Jersey's response team in efficiently prioritizing and addressing residents' urgent messages. These stories fulfill fundamental human needs for belonging and significance, instilling pride in your team and enhancing their commitment to customer success.

Frame your sales team goals: Action and urgency

Sales is a highly performance-driven profession with frequent measurements and public disclosures of metrics. While sales goals are essential, framing them is crucial for inspiring action instead of instilling fear in your team. The language used should convey the importance of goals beyond meeting quotas or avoiding reprimands. Framing involves positioning goals in the context of making a difference to customers. For instance, emphasizing the need to help 5,000 new customers rather than adding $100 million in revenue. This approach influences the feelings and beliefs of the team, reducing quota anxiety and fostering commitment to meaningful objectives within their control.

Go beyond numbers in pipeline reviews

Enhance your pipeline reviews by going beyond the standard questions of when and how much. Elevate the process by delving into the five categories of critical customer information: the customer's environment, goals, challenges, success metrics, and potential consequences of failure. This comprehensive approach, focused on understanding the customer, provides valuable insights that can increase your reps' skills and emotional engagement. Additionally, it aids in avoiding overconfidence in deal projections and aligns your team with the customer impact perspective, fostering stronger relationships and strategic selling.

Deliver performance reviews that drive results

Transform performance reviews into meaningful conversations that focus on ongoing development rather than shaming for quota shortcomings. Before addressing performance challenges, ask crucial questions: Does the person have adequate training, necessary resources, and essential support? Ensure your rep is equipped for success. After identifying areas for improvement, create a plan with clear next steps, whether it involves additional training, coaching, or procedural adjustments. Recognize and highlight positive aspects of their performance, encouraging them to replicate successful practices. Conduct regular, proactive conversations with your team, avoiding surprises during yearly reviews. Be a supportive leader, not a source of anxiety.

Motivating a sales rep before a big call

While preparing a sales rep for a significant call, avoid excessive rehearsing that may lead to scripted interactions. Instead, focus on grounding them in a value case, emphasizing the five categories of critical customer intelligence: customer's environment, goals, challenges, success, and lack of success. This information should shape the rep's pitch and serve as the foundation for pre-call homework and discovery questions. Motivate your rep by asking them to consider the scenario of the customer saying no, enabling them to anticipate obstacles and plan responses. Be conscious of the timeline, offering robust feedback when there's sufficient preparation time. This proactive approach allows you to game plan, coach, and reinforce the importance of making a difference to customers.

What to say to a rep 10 minutes before a big sales call

In the critical moments before a significant sales call, a sales leader's words set the tone for the conversation. Instead of delving into small details or emphasizing high stakes, focus on maximizing this brief window by directing the sales rep's attention to ultimate customer impact. Ask the game-changing question: "How will this customer be different as a result of doing business with us?" Encourage the rep to articulate the impact on the customer's business, ensuring a true north of customer-centricity. Validate their response, expand positively, and keep them grounded in what matters to the customer. This approach leverages the short timeframe effectively, guiding the rep toward making a difference to customers, the key to sealing the deal.

Micro-motivation: Upping enthusiasm in 10 seconds

For a quick motivational boost, especially with a large or time-strapped team, focus on physiological cues rather than lengthy speeches. In a brief timeframe, prompt your sales rep to take a deep breath, sending oxygen to their brain for improved focus and strategic thinking. Remind them of their noble purpose — making a difference for the person they're about to engage with. This shifts their brain toward serotonin, fostering a lasting sense of worthiness, belonging, and self-esteem. Unlike the short-lived dopamine-driven motivation, serotonin aligns with long-term accomplishments, ensuring lasting results and preventing burnout. The goal is to relax your rep and connect them to a noble purpose in those crucial seconds before a sales call.

Help a sales rep rebound from a loss

Most organizations tend to overlook losses, rushing to the next deal. However, strategic sales teams recognize the value of loss reviews, understanding the lessons for future success. While these reviews can be uncomfortable, they can also be motivational when anchored in a sense of purpose. Basic loss review questions include why a deal didn't close and if key decision-makers were engaged. To elevate it to a motivational level, end with three questions: "What's the most impactful sale we've ever made?" "Why did it matter to the customer?" and "How can we do it again?" This approach brings energy and motivation back after a potentially uncomfortable conversation. The focus shifts from what went wrong to learning and improvement.

Build on success: How to recreate a win

Celebrating a win is a perfect time to boost motivation and channel success into future activities. After the happy dance, engage in a motivating conversation with your rep. Ask them three crucial questions: 1) What are they most proud of in how they handled the sale? 2) Is there anything they wish they'd done differently or more of? 3) What excites them most for the customer? These questions help the rep recognize their role in the win, identify opportunities for growth, and emphasize the positive impact on the customer. The goal is to set the rep up for future success by reinforcing their confidence and highlighting the customer's benefit.

Enable your team to recover from setbacks

When your team faces challenges like a bad quarter or losing a big customer, it's crucial to provide a reset. Instead of focusing solely on the next deal or product update, consider the difference between passion and purpose. Passion is personal excitement, while purpose is the belief that your work contributes to others. Research indicates that purpose beats passion in driving job performance. Employees with a strong sense of purpose outperform those with passion but no purpose. As a motivational sales leader, recalibrate your team by emphasizing the impact they have on customers. Remind them of significant wins, share examples of positive impacts, and highlight opportunities to make a difference. This focus on purpose fosters resilience and helps the team rebound after setbacks.

Spotlight team success without playing favorites

Celebrating team success is vital for maintaining momentum and morale. Beyond closing deals, strategic motivational sales leaders recognize and applaud key behaviors that contribute to long-term success. These include a focus on continuous learning, efforts to recover from setbacks, honing essential sales skills, and being a supportive teammate. By highlighting these behaviors, leaders reinforce the importance of ongoing improvement, resilience, and collaboration, fostering a positive team culture that goes beyond just winning big deals.

Manage team turnover

Sales team turnover can be challenging for leaders, both emotionally and logistically. To minimize turnover, ensure competitive compensation, benefits, learning opportunities, and a positive work culture. Regular check-ins with team members about job satisfaction and growth aspirations are crucial. Address subtle signs of disengagement promptly. When turnover occurs, maintain respect and inquire about the departure professionally. Emphasize appreciation for the departing employee's contributions and highlight their impact on customers and the team. This approach fosters a positive employer brand and reinforces the importance of making a difference within the organization.

Declare your sales culture to win more talent

A compelling sales team culture is essential for attracting and retaining top talent. To differentiate your organization, emphasize how your team makes a difference to customers, providing specific examples. Highlight growth opportunities, including advancement, new projects, and continuous learning. Explicitly communicate your purpose-driven culture in job postings, ensuring it stands out among competitors. During interviews, assess candidates' alignment with your culture. Leverage the power of employee referrals, as those who have experienced your culture firsthand can authentically promote it. Clearly communicate your motivating, purpose-driven culture to both customers and potential hires.

Continuing to grow your sales leadership skills

Your words as a sales leader hold significant power to inspire and elevate your team's enthusiasm. A motivated and inspired team performs better and finds greater enjoyment in their work. Sales, at its core, is a noble profession focused on enhancing the lives of customers. Reject the notion that you must choose between financial success and making a positive impact—you can achieve both, and you and your team deserve it.

Utilize this guide during pipeline reviews to delve into crucial customer information across five categories:

1. Customer Environment:

   - Organization dynamics

   - Competing priorities

   - Market position

- Political landscape within the organization

2. Customer Goals:

  - Objectives

  - Measurement criteria

  - Progress with current goals

  - Leadership's priorities

3. Customer Challenges:

  - Obstacles faced

  - Concerns and issues

  - Resource availability and needs

4. Success Definition for the Customer:

  - How success is defined and measured

  - Recognition of success by your contact

  - Boss's criteria for success

5. Lack of Success for the Customer:

  - Customer's fears

  - Organizational consequences of failure

  - Impact on your contact

If time is limited, employ the key question: "How will this customer be different as a result of doing business with us?" This question redirects focus towards customer impact and success, transcending mere deal considerations.